Great Annuals

From Bud to Seed

Great Annuals
Photographs by Carol Sharp
Words by Clare Foster

From Bud to Seed

conran

OCTOPUS

First published in 2001 by Conran Octopus Limited
a part of Octopus Publishing Group
2–4 Heron Quays, London E14 4JP
www.conran-octopus.co.uk

Publishing Director Lorraine Dickey
Senior Editor Muna Reyal
Editor Galiena Hitchman

Creative Director Leslie Harrington
Executive Art Editor Megan Smith
Designer Caz Hildebrand

Production Director Zoe Fawcett
Senior Production Controller Manjit Sihra

British Library Cataloguing-in-Publication Data.
A catalogue record for this book is available from the British Library.

ISBN 1 84091 190 5

Colour origination by Sang Choy International, Singapore

Printed in China

Contents

Foreword by Carol Sharp

My garden is my sanctuary. It is also my studio and a canvas for my passion – plants. I have gradually filled it with plants that fascinate me in all their stages. I've noticed I am drawn continually over the year to those that have more than just a glorious flower; some plants have intriguing buds and seedheads and even interest in the foliage, which may often change colour over the seasons.

By continually photographing them in different lights and from different angles I have to look and look again, and still I see more. The closer I get the more is revealed, the lens unveiling much more than you can see with the naked eye. As I wander among them I watch their characters emerge – changing every day, as they perform their part in the great theatre of the garden. To do justice to the drama I see unfolding, I have decided to present them in four main scenes.

Scene One: Bud The bud has an exquisite secret which makes it all the more alluring. It is usually green but bursting with promise of the colour that is yet to come.

Scene Two: Bloom The flower is the peak of the performance: whether unassuming or exuberant, a flower always fills me with intense joy. The rich variation of shapes and colours never cease to amaze me. Looking closer the petals lead you to the centre and the intricate design of the stamens and stigma.

Scene Three: Foliage Although the leaves are first to appear, they play a supporting role and must wait until Scene Three to take centre stage. While lacking the drama of the bud or bloom, the leaves often have special interest and provide a sound structure for the main performers.

Scene Four: Seed The vehicle the plant has devised to disperse its seeds often appears to echo the flower in a very avant-garde way. This is often my favourite part of the performance.

No two years' performance will be the same, as the conditions vary from year to year, and although every year I anticipate each stage, it is still with a sense of wonder that I see the constant cycle of growth unfold, marking the passage of time in the garden.

A year in the garden

Most of the annuals in this book have never needed re-sowing in my garden as, apart from the sunflower, spider flower and the castor-oil plant, they faithfully reappear from autumn, self-sown. January brings frosts and their emerging foliage is tested. Some of them will not make it, but there are usually new seeds waiting under the surface. White skeletons of the silvery discs of the biennial honesty, torn away by birds feasting on the seeds, are still braving the winter. I notice the new plants established from last year are knee high by February. The clary sage is also biennial and its huge furry leaves fill the spaces in the borders left by the hibernating perennials.

In March I capture the love-in-a-mist foliage, now a bright green fuzzy carpet, and in April the leaves of the opium poppies that have made it through the mild winter, which are whorls of grey. The reliable little candytuft flowers in May as does the honesty, a welcome mass of bright pink as I sow the later-flowering plants. The pointed hats of the Californian poppy are pushed higher and higher until they topple off and the bright orange flowers burst forth: a delight to photograph in June. The buds of the opium poppy have got so fat they are splitting and the crinkled petals unfurl to reveal unexpected variations, sometimes double, always glorious. I choose a double for the shot.

Throughout the summer drifts of love-in-a-mist are alight with their unusual flowers. I photograph them in the shade when the sky is blue to get the intensity of their colour. With the borage I decide the backlight of the sun shows the hairiness up best. In July I keep an eye on the castor-oil plant as the frothy cream flowers do not last long; but I can shoot bud, flower and seedhead on the same plant as it gets bigger. The sunflower has shot up with it and its dark flower nods down in a complementary colour during August. September brings quite a different colour – the deep magenta of the extraordinary, exotic spider flower. I tear myself away to capture the clary sage, now covered with tiny hook-shaped white flowers. Both go on flowering into October, sometimes November. Up until the first frosts borage, which takes only six weeks from germination, has re-sown itself and continues to flower, as does love-in-a-mist and the Californian poppy.

By December the silvery pods of the honesty dominate the garden, but below them the seedlings of the hardy annuals are already pushing up for another season.

Introduction

Annuals appeal to those who like quick results. Growing extremely swiftly from seed, they flower sometimes within six weeks of germination – but they will only live for a single year, blooming for one season before dying. Similarly, biennials flower only once, but the year after the seed has germinated, so their life cycle is over two years, not one. To confuse matters further, some plants grow naturally as perennials (for example the castor-oil plant, *Ricinus communis*), but are grown in temperate climates as annuals, so for all intents and purposes they are referred to as annuals.

Annuals have had a bad press from the garish colours, orderly rows and blocks of the 'bedding schemes' favoured through much of the twentieth century, but having thrown off their old image, they are enjoying a come back. Despite their short lives annuals are appreciated for their versatility and variety in shape, colour and texture. Tall or short, climbing or ground-covering, there are annuals for every situation from sun to shade. Most annuals are grown for their bright, cheerful flowers, often sweetly scented, but many people ignore the spring foliage and autumn seedheads, both of which can be spectacular. Mixed with perennials and shrubs, annuals quickly provide vibrant displays of colour – perhaps to fill in a gap later to be taken by a slower-developing perennial, or in containers for instant plant gratification. There are thousands of genera and species to choose from, and even more varieties (cultivars) that have been bred artificially by nurserymen, and we hope that this small selection will whet the appetite to use these versatile plants to their full potential.

A note on plant names
The nomenclature of plants can be confusing. Often, the Latin botanical name (genus plus species, for example *Helianthus annuus*) is supplemented by a common name (in this instance 'sunflower') which can vary from country to country, even region to region. To complicate things further, if the plant is a cultivated version of the species (cultivar), it will have another name added after the genus and species, for example *Helianthus annuus* 'Velvet Queen'. In this book, we have used the common name as far as possible, although if we are referring to a specific cultivar we have used the full Latin name plus cultivar.

Opium poppy
Papaver somniferum

Bud

The bud of the opium poppy, about the size of a quail's egg, droops demurely downwards before turning its petals up to the sun.

With flowers like ruffled silk and leaves that feel like moleskin, the opium poppy is the *crème de la crème* of the poppy family. The wild form bears single mauve blooms in summer, but there are hundreds of variations on the original theme in shades of pink, purple and cream, with double as well as single blooms (the doubles are often known as 'peony-flowered'). The beautiful, pale blue-grey leaves are themselves a talking point in early spring, while the late summer seedheads are almost as seductive as the flowers – large, grey-green globes that mature to an antique brown.

'Like a burning coal fallen from heaven's altars'
JOHN RUSKIN

Despite its innocent appearance, the opium poppy is a powerful enchantress. Since 3400BC, when it was first grown by the Sumerians as the 'joy plant', it has been cultivated legally as a source of morphine and codeine, and illegally to produce the drugs opium and heroin. The crucial alkaloids are contained in a white latex produced when the unripe seed capsules are cut, giving the plant its botanical name, from the Latin *papilla* or breast. Opium is the name given to the dried latex, and is well known for its strongly addictive nature and narcotic effects. Although opium is today regarded as a dangerously addictive drug, morphine and codeine have been used in medicine for thousands of years. The Greek physician Dioscorides noted that 'a decoction of the leaves and flowerhead... is unrivalled in inducing sleep', while Hippocrates acknowledged opium's usefulness in treating internal diseases and epidemics. In the sixteenth century, opium was made into little black pills known as 'Stones of Immortality'. The seeds of the opium poppy can be used on bread and cakes to impart a slightly nutty flavour, and oil from the seeds is extracted to make salad dressings.

Bloom

The stunning bowl-shaped flowers of the opium poppy, up to 10cm (4in) across, come in a wide range of colours and are a delightful addition to any summer border.

Foliage

Unlike many other poppies, the foliage of the opium poppy is an attraction in itself, acting out its own prelude before the flowers have appeared. Deeply lobed, the leaves can grow up to 13cm (5in) long.

Seed

The opium poppy has wonderful, bloated seed pods that are often dried for flower arrangements. As the plant matures, the small black seeds can be heard rattling around inside the pepper-pot capsule.

Height 1.2m (4ft)
Spread 30cm (12in)

Cultivation
Grow the opium poppy in full sun in fertile, well-drained soil. It is a hardy annual.

Propagation
Sow *in situ* in spring by broadcasting seed and then raking it gently in.

Pests and diseases
The opium poppy is mostly trouble free, but it can occasionally suffer from aphid infestation or mildew if the conditions are wet.

Associations
Grow the opium poppy in an informal border or a meadow along with other cornfield annuals such as cornflowers (*Centaurea cyanus*) and corn chamomile (*Anthemis arvensis*).

Love-in-a-mist

Nigella damascena

Bud

Peeping up through a mass of young green foliage, the bud of love-in-a-mist is like a precious gemstone.

Nigella damascena is a plant with a split personality. Its jewel-like flowers, shrouded modestly in a mist of ferny foliage, gave rise to the lyrical name 'love-in-a-mist', while the curious seedheads with spiky 'horns' are the reason for its other, very different name, 'devil-in-a-bush'. But whichever way you look at it, this is a charming plant, creating soft, fluid lines in the summer border with clouds of emerald-green foliage and sapphire-blue flowers. The fat seedheads are equally attractive, like green and pink-striped pantaloons, and they contain small, black, aromatic seeds that give the plant its botanical name, from the Latin word *niger*, meaning black. For centuries, these and the seeds of *N. sativa*, have been used for flavouring food, and today the seeds are still used in bread, cakes and curries.

'Love's not time's fool'

SHAKESPEARE

Love-in-a-mist has attracted attention from both literary and artistic worlds. Karl Blossfeldt photographed the graphic seedhead in black and white, while the Belgian poet Maurice Maeterlinck eulogized the plant in a lyrical essay: 'At the source of the flower, the five extremely long pistils stand close-grouped in the centre of the azure crown, like five queens clad in green gowns, haughty and inaccessible. Around them crowd hopelessly the innumerable throng of their lovers, the stamens... At a given moment, as though obeying the secret and irresistible command of love, they all together bend backwards and gracefully cull the golden dust of the nuptial kiss on the lips of their humble lovers.'

Love-in-a-mist is most at home in Mediterranean-like conditions. Several good cultivars are available, and the best-loved of these has to be 'Miss Jekyll', discovered by Gertrude Jekyll in Kent, who described it as being 'of an unusually fine colour'. 'Oxford Blue' is a darker blue, while 'Miss Jekyll Rose' is a pretty pink.

Bloom

As delicate as a butterfly's wing, the exquisite flowers of love-in-a-mist can grow up to 4.5cm (1¾ in) across. They appear in early summer, pale blue at first, darkening with age.

Foliage

In the spring border, the soft foliage of love-in-a-mist contrasts well with larger-leaved plants. The foliage extends up towards the flowers, where it creates a ferny ruff around the petals.

Seed

Love-in-a-mist has large, candy-striped seed pods that are just as attractive as the flowers. Maturing to an attractive papery brown, they should be left to decay gracefully, adding interest to the autumn garden.

Height to 50cm (20in)
Spread to 23cm (9in)

Cultivation
Being Mediterranean in origin, love-in-a-mist isn't too fussy about soil type, but good drainage is essential. It should be grown in full sun.

Propagation
Love-in-a-mist is a hardy annual and the seed can be sown either in early autumn or early spring. Sow *in situ* in short drills 1cm (½in) deep, and thin the seedlings as required.

Pests and diseases
Trouble free.

Associations
The fine foliage and delicate flowers of love-in-a-mist look best with plants with larger leaves such as euphorbias, arum lilies or irises.

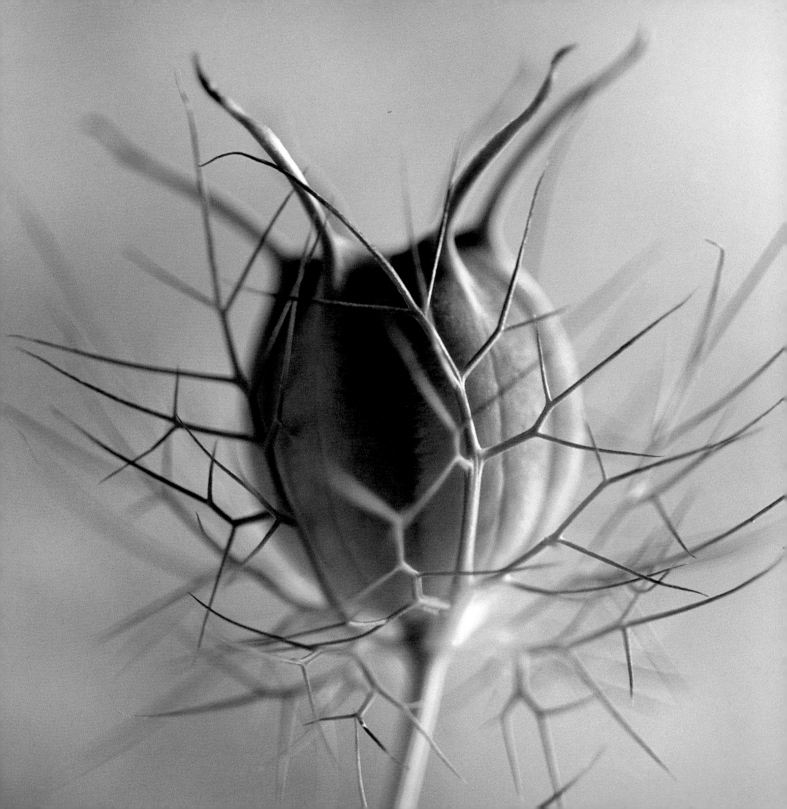

Candytuft

Iberis umbellata

Bud

*Candytuft's neatly
clustered pale green
buds appear in late
spring. Each nodule will
yield a tiny flower.*

A sweetly scented confection of frothy flowers, candytuft is one of the prettiest plants in the garden and one of the most rewarding annuals to grow. Although diminutive in size, it works well at the front of a border or a rock garden, and is always eager to please, even when growing in poor soil. Flowering from early summer onwards in pretty pastel shades of pink, mauve and white, it produces compact mounds of lacy, perfumed blooms – if you look closely, you will notice that each 'flower' is actually a mass of tiny flowers, each with four petals, crowded together in a perfect arrangement to form a dense cluster.

'The sweetest thing in nature'
CHARLES LAMB

Iberis umbellata, also known as common or globe candytuft, is one of 40 species in the genus and a member of the cabbage family *(Brassicaceae)*. The Latin name relates to the plant's Mediterranean origins, while the common name, although appropriately conveying the nature of the plant, is said to be derived from the word Candia, an old name for the island of Crete. In the wild, iberis grows in dry, limey soil, and for the best results these conditions should be mimicked in cultivation. Two sets of cultivars are readily available, offering a mixed palette of colour within the same growth: the 'Flash' series have vibrant pink, purple or red flowers, while the 'Fairy' series have paler white, pink or lilac flowers.

Candytuft was a popular Victorian bedding plant, favoured by William Robinson as 'the most useful of annual flowers' and used by Gertrude Jekyll in her many inspired spring and summer planting schemes. William Robinson also praises the rocket candytuft, *I. amara*, whose white, frothy flowers are held on elongated, domed spires, and *I. sempervirens*, a perennial candytuft with darker leaves than the annual species, whose white flowers appear in May and June.

Bloom

Candytuft's white, pink or mauve flowers are grouped together in neat, rounded half-domes up to 5cm (2in) across, and when fully out, form a dense cloud which all but obscures the foliage underneath. The sweet, musky scent is attractive to bees and butterflies as well as humans.

Foliage

*Candytuft bears long,
thin, sword-like leaves
up to 10cm (4in) long
that act as a kind of
scaffolding for the
froth of flowers.*

Height 15–30cm (6–12in)
Spread to 23cm (9in)

Cultivation
Grow candytuft in an open spot in full sun. It is not fussy about soil type, although adding extra manure or compost before planting will help keep moisture in and reduce the need for watering in summer. It is a hardy annual.

Propagation
Sow seed *in situ* either in autumn or early spring. Sow in drills 1cm (½in)deep and cover with finely raked soil. When seedlings appear 2–3 weeks later, thin out so that plants are about 10cm (4in) apart.

Pests and diseases
Candytuft is a brassica, and can suffer from clubroot just as cabbages do. There is no treatment, although replanting pot-sown specimens among affected plants will help support them and encourage them to flower.

Associations
Grow as a bedding plant at the front of a border, with lobelia and white petunias, flanked perhaps by the silver leaves of *Convolvulus cneorum*. Gertrude Jekyll suggested planting it with white tulips and the small shrub *Lithodora diffusa*.

Seed

The candelabra seedheads of Candytuft contain filmy pods, each with two or three seeds.

Castor-oil plant
Ricinus communis 'Carmencita'

Bud

The buds of this plant appear with very little warning from below the leaves. A hermaphrodite, the castor-oil plant contains both male and female components, and it is the female flowers that emerge first from the bud. The male flowers appear a few days later.

Castor oil may be one of those childhood memories that you'd prefer to forget, yet its source is a plant that graces many gardens. One of history's oldest cultivated plants, *Ricinus communis* was first grown 6,000 years ago by the Ancient Egyptians, who used oil from the seeds for lamps and cosmetics. Today the oil still has many uses – medicinally it acts as a purgative and can relieve constipation, and it is sometimes used to induce birth. It can also be found in many common household goods, from soap and emollients to candles and fabric dyes. However, it is in the ornamental garden that this plant is most valued and admired. The castor-oil plant is a fast-growing, seed-raised tender annual that will flourish in temperate climates outside its native Africa and Asia.

'Big, bold and beautiful'
GRAHAM RICE, *Discovering Annuals*

Despite its exuberant appearance, the castor-oil plant is the *femme fatale* of the garden and beneath all its architectural splendour is a far darker side. The seeds, enclosed within spherical seed capsules, contain a deadly poison that gained notoriety in the 1970s after an impregnated umbrella tip was employed in a political assassination. The seeds are so poisonous that eating just two of them could prove fatal. Handled with care, however, this is an extremely rewarding plant to grow. If you have plenty of space, why not plant a whole grove of castor-oil plants, using a range of cultivars with different leaf colours, from the deep vibrant red of 'Carmencita' to the grey-green of 'Zanzibariensis'? To get the best results, raise the seedlings in a heated greenhouse or even indoors on a window-sill, and plant out when all danger of frost has passed. Then all that remains is to watch the plants getting bigger each day – in a long, warm summer, they could reach a height of 2m (6ft) or more.

Bloom

The flowers of the castor-oil plant aren't the focal point, but they are nonetheless interesting. Appearing on spikes from the central stem, the clusters of tiny greenish-white flowers are the male part of the plant, while the red stigma above constitute the female part. Seed capsules will start forming while the plant is still flowering, so there can be three distinctive components to the flower spike.

Foliage

The palmate leaves of the castor-oil plant are its raison d'etre *in the ornamental garden. Ranging from dark red or bronzy purple to mid-green, the leaves have 5–12 lobes and can be as large as 45cm (18in) long. They are fragile, their central veins easily broken, so shelter should be provided from strong winds.*

Height to 1.8m (6ft)
Spread 1m (3ft)

Cultivation

The castor-oil plant should be grown in an open, sunny position in well-drained, humus-rich soil that has been well manured. A liquid feed during the summer will ensure rapid and lush growth. The leaves are fragile, so shelter from strong winds is necessary. The plant can also be grown in a greenhouse for extra protection.

Propagation

Grow from seed in early spring by soaking the seed overnight in warm water, and then planting a single seed in a 7cm (2¾ in) pot. Keep indoors or in a heated greenhouse at a temperature of 21°C (70°F). As the seedling gets bigger, pot on into larger pots, until the plant has filled a 20cm (8in) pot. As it is only half hardy, it should only be planted out when all danger of frost has passed.

Pests and diseases

The leaves can be affected by red spider mite, particularly if grown under glass. Wiping the leaves with a damp cloth every day can help relieve the problem.

Associations

With its large glossy leaves, the castor-oil plant is a good addition to a border full of architectural or exotic plants. Graham Rice advises planting it with bright climbing nasturtiums or black-eyed Susan to contrast with the dark leaves.

Seed

The female flowers develop into alluring seed capsules in autumn. Covered with soft, reddish-brown spines, they contain seeds the size of kidney beans. The source of castor oil, these seeds must nevertheless be treated with caution as they contain a toxic poison called ricin that can be fatal if ingested.

Sunflower

Helianthus annuus 'Velvet Queen'

Bud

From the moment they emerge in spring, sunflowers are fun to watch. Protected by spiny bracts, the large bud appears in midsummer, reaching up towards the sun as if needing the energy to open the flower.

Known and loved by millions for its cheerful yellow flowerheads, the sunflower is the Eliza Dolittle of the garden. Common it may be, but throughout the ages the sunflower has always been something of an icon. Native to the Americas, it was held in high esteem by Incan priests as a symbol of the sun god, and when it was introduced into Europe in the 1500s, it was used to decorate the church on St Bartholomew's day, representing constancy and devotion. Later still, the sunflower was immortalized by Vincent Van Gogh in his paintings, as a symbol of light, renewal and health. On a more practical level, sunflower seeds have been a source of food for thousands of years, and are still used today in health foods, cooking oil and margarine. The native Americans ground the seeds up to make a dye, while the fibres from the stem were used in basketry and weaving. Various medicinal uses of the seeds have been recorded – in Iowa they were mixed with sugar to make a syrup for whooping cough, and in Norway, a bag of seeds around the neck was said to keep smallpox away.

'Light-enchanted sunflower!'
PERCY BYSSHE SHELLEY

Since Van Gogh's time, the sunflower has evolved enormously, with many new cultivars taking the plant into a different realm. No longer do sunflowers have to be yellow. The wonderful 'Velvet Queen' variety is rusty-red, while 'Moonwalker' has very pale yellow flowers. There are dwarf varieties, pollen-free cultivars, and even 'hedging sunflowers'. Extremely easy to cultivate, sunflowers require little attention apart from watering in spells of hot weather – but if you are hoping to beat your neighbour in terms of height, an open sunny spot with well-manured, rich soil is advisable, as this will ensure rapid growth. The world record height for a sunflower is a gigantic 7.7m (25½ft).

Bloom

The richly coloured blooms of 'Velvet Queen' can grow up to 20cm (8in) in diameter. The flower is daisy-like, with outer rays and a central brown disc.

Foliage

*In the right conditions,
the foliage of the
sunflower grows
remarkably quickly from
a sturdy stem. The
heart-shaped leaves
can grow up to
40cm (16in) long.*

Height to 5m (16ft)
Spread to 60cm (2ft)

Cultivation

Hot, sunny conditions are essential if the sunflower is to grow to a good size. Watering is needed when the weather is dry. If you are growing tall forms, cane supports may be needed. Sunflowers are hardy annuals.

Propagation

Plant seed *in situ* in well-manured or composted soil in early spring, putting three seeds in together and later removing the two weaker seedlings. Alternatively, plant in pots outside and transplant when the seedlings are big enough.

Pests and diseases

Sunflowers are, on the whole, trouble free.

Associations

Because they are so tall, sunflowers are usually grown as separate entities rather than in a combination with other plants. They look good next to a south-facing wall, at the back of a large border, or even in a row to brighten up a vegetable plot.

Seed

The sunflower's central disc becomes the seedhead in autumn. Sturdy and long-lasting, it dries to a dark brown and becomes a welcome meal for birds during the colder months.

Spider flower

Cleome hassleriana 'Violet Queen'

Bud

The delicate buds of the spider flower are green at first, turning to dark magenta pink before spreading open into small, pinkish flowers.

With a flowerhead like an exploding firework, the spider flower is an exotic and eye-catching addition to an informal border. Widely cultivated in North America for 200 years, it has only recently become popular in British gardens, always attracting attention when grown with more traditional border plants. Fast-growing and trouble free, the plants need a good deal of elbow room to reach their full potential and, given a long, warm summer, they will reach heights of up to 1.5m (5ft). The flowers release a sweet, musky scent, and the leaves are also pungent – in fact mildly unpleasant to some, leading to various names such as the skunk plant.

'The spider's touch, how exquisitely fine!'
ALEXANDER POPE

Cleome hassleriana is one of 120 species of cleome, native to tropical and sub-tropical areas worldwide, growing best in sandy, well-drained soil in a sunny, humid climate. Various colour forms are available including 'Violet Queen', 'Cherry Queen' and the pure white 'Helen Campbell'. A mixture called 'Colour Fountain' is also available, offering a good range of pinks, purples and mauves that blend into an abundant summer border. Close cousins, *C. lutea*, the yellow beeplant, and *C. serrulata*, the Rocky Mountain beeplant, have spread through North America, growing wild along the west coast. They were put to a variety of practical uses by the native Americans – the leaves, rich in vitamin A and iron, were boiled and eaten, while the seeds were ground with corn to make bread. The leaves were also used to make a poultice to treat ant bites, and the flowers of *C. lutea* yield a blackish pigment that was used to paint pottery. The Navajo indians made a decoction of the seeds for 'good blood' and for improving the voice, and a cold infusion of the leaves can be used as a body deodorant or to treat fungal infections such as athlete's foot.

Bloom

The spider flower blooms over a long period in summer, forming large globe-like clusters of small four-petalled flowers whose sweet scent is attractive to bees. The flowerheads, about 7½ cm (3in) across, incorporate many long thread-like stamens. See page 92 for the white variety 'Helen Campbell'.

Foliage

Growing up to 13cm (5in) long, the palmate leaves of the spider flower add to the exotic character of the plant – but beware, each leaf bears an unexpected and very sharp spine at the base where it joins the stem.

Seed

The spider flower forms long, slim seed pods on stalks, each with a generous portion of seeds that can be collected for next year's seedlings.

Height to 1.5m (5ft)
Spread 45cm (18in)

Cultivation
Grow the spider flower in full sun in a well-drained site. For swift growth, dig in well-rotted manure or compost. Native to the tropics, the plant is half hardy.

Propagation
Sow seeds in 9cm (3½in) pots in early spring, and keep under glass or indoors at 18°C (65°F). The seedlings should be hardened off before planting out in late spring when all danger of frost has passed.

Pests and diseases
Aphids can be a nuisance, particularly with young plants, causing twisted growth.

Associations
Spider flowers mix particularly well with cosmos, with flowers in the same colour range, and the plant is a good bushy filler for a large border. It also looks good with other exotic-looking plants such as cannas and *Melianthus major*.

Clary sage
Salvia sclarea var. turkestanica

Bud

*Like a crayfish tail,
the bud of clary sage
consists of a series of
green-edged pink bracts
from which the tall flower
spike emerges.*

Gently healing, aromatic and soothing, salvias have been used for thousands of years in domestic remedies to treat everything from indigestion to consumption. According to legend, the plant's medicinal power was the result of a blessing from the Virgin Mary, who had hidden beneath a salvia bush during the flight from Egypt. The name, too, relates to the healing strengths of the plant, derived from the Latin *salveo*, to be in good health, and the plant was so highly revered that an old Latin proverb asked 'How can a man die who grows sage in his garden?'

'A nobly architectural plant'
CHRISTOPHER LLOYD

Clary sage is just one of a staggering 900 species in the genus, a sun-loving biennial native to southern Europe and the Middle East. It produces low rosettes of leaves in the first year, and then sends up tall spikes of mauve flowers the following season, flowering in midsummer until well into autumn – an ideal structural filler. The turkestanica variety is even lovelier than the species, with pink stems, pale pink flowers and stunning lilac bracts flecked with pink, creating a mound of hazy colour ideal for the back of a border or herb garden.

Today clary sage is used in herbal medicine for stomach problems, premenstrual tension and menopausal complaints. Also known as 'clear eye', the seeds were once used to treat eye problems. Like its close cousin, common sage (*S. officinalis*), it is a useful culinary herb, its mild-tasting leaves used to flavour meat dishes, in salads or to make fritters. The flowers are also edible, and can be a decorative addition to a salad, or used to make a soothing herbal tea.

The plant is grown commercially in France and Russia for its essential oil; the crop in flower must be a beautiful sight. Used in aromatherapy, the musk-scented, pale yellow oil is obtained from the leaves and flowers.

Bloom

Lilac to sweet candyfloss pink, the flowers of clary sage are small 2cm (¾in) blooms, cradled by petal-like bracts, all the way up tall flower spikes. The spikes can be used as cut flowers and are also used in dried flower arrangements.

Foliage

The heart-shaped leaves of clary sage are crinkled, soft and felt-like, growing around the base of the plant. Aromatically scented and flavoured, they can be used for culinary purposes.

Height 1.5m (5ft)
Spread 30cm (12in)

Cultivation
Grow clary sage in an open, sunny position in well-drained soil. In the right conditions, this plant will need little attention.

Propagation
Sow seed in 9cm (3½ in) pots as soon as ripe in summer, and keep in a cold frame or greenhouse over winter. Alternatively, plant *in situ* in spring after all danger of frost has passed.

Pests and diseases
Young growth is susceptible to snail and slug damage.

Associations
Clary sage associates well with other sun-loving aromatic plants such as lavender and santolina. Try it with some of the many other salvias, such as the rich 'Mainacht', or with other similar shaped and coloured plants such as *Agastache foeniculum* and *Veronicastrum virginicum roseum*.

Seed

At the end of summer, the small flowers of clary sage shrivel and fall away, leaving small seed pods filled with seed. The pink bracts remain intact, drying to an attractive nutty brown.

Borage

Borago officinalis

Bud

After swift spring growth, small clusters of pretty candy-striped buds appear in summer, slowly opening up into clear blue star-shaped flowers.

'I, Borage, bring always courage'
ANCIENT LATIN SAYING

Easily grown from seed, borage is a trouble free and congenial addition to a herb garden, and also makes a good companion plant in a vegetable plot, attracting bees and luring blackfly away from the rest of the crops. It may be an unremarkable plant on first sight, with small flowers and a rather rangy habit, but once you get to know it you will realize there is more to it than meets the eye. Although it grows as a weed in many parts of the Mediterranean, it is widely cultivated as a herb, grown for its leaves and flowers which are used to flavour drinks and salads with their pleasantly cucumbery flavour. It also has medicinal value. The leaves are a diuretic and the flowers encourage sweating, thereby helping to reduce high temperatures, while oil from the seeds is also used to treat premenstrual complaints and rheumatism. It is also a good emolient, making it a useful treatment for sore and inflamed skin, including eczema.

Borage has been highly valued since Greek and Roman times, when it was believed to impart courage to anyone who ate it. Later, during the Crusades, warriors drank from cups with borage flowers floating in them to make them brave in battle. By the seventeenth century, borage was used as a kind of anti-depressant. John Gerard proclaimed that it would 'drive away sorrow and increase the joy of the mind', while John Evelyn wrote that it was 'of known virtue to revive the hypochondriac and cheer the hard student'.

There are several theories for the derivation of the botanical name. One is that it comes from the Latin *burra*, a word for a hairy garment, relating to the plant's hairy stems and leaves, while the other more plausible derivation is from the Celtic word *borrach*, meaning courage.

Bloom

*Although small in size –
up to 2.5cm (1in) across
– the intense blue of the
borage flower is the
plant's star attraction.
Hanging down on
nodding stems, the
flowers appear in early
summer and last for a
long period, sometimes
up until the first frosts.
They can be used in
salads, in summer drinks,
or even crystallized for a
cake decoration.*

Foliage

*Don't let the hairy, even
slightly prickly, texture of
a borage leaf put you off.
If eaten, the hairs quickly
dissolve on the tongue
and the leaf will impart its
pleasant cucumbery
taste. The leaves can be
chopped up in salads,
mixed with soft cheese,
or added to cold summer
drinks such as Pimm's.*

Height 60cm (24in)
Spread 45cm (18in)

Cultivation

Plant borage seed *in situ* in mid spring. Soil should be well-drained, and not too rich, and the site sunny. The plant needs little maintenance, but should be deadheaded every now and then to prolong the flowering period. Pick flowers and leaves throughout the summer for culinary purposes.

Propagation

Sow seed 5cm (2in) deep in mid spring. Thin the seedlings to 60cm (24in) apart, as they produce lots of leafy growth.

Pests and diseases

The main problem is blackfly, but if you are growing it as a companion plant, then this is a good thing. If it starts to take over, spray with horticultural soap.

Associations

Because it attracts bees, borage is a good companion for crops needing pollination, such as runner beans and strawberries. It also grows well with almost any other herb.

Seed

When the flowers disappear, the borage plant dries to a mellow brown. The hairy seedheads, still nodding downwards, contain copious seeds that will germinate readily next spring.

Californian poppy

Eschscholzia californica

Bud

Like tightly furled parasols, the buds of the Californian poppy stand proud on top of 30cm (12in) stems. The delicate sheaths protecting them will soon split as the petals unfold little by little in the warmth of the sun.

Always bright and cheerful, the Californian poppy is one of the easiest-going annuals around, its delicate orange flowers bringing an undeniable lift to the garden. As you might expect from a native of California, it thrives in full sun, and being an undemanding type it actually prefers a poor, dry soil – a very rich soil will encourage too much leafy growth at the expense of the flowers. The simple, delicate flowers, which are predominantly orange but sometimes yellow, white or red, appear in spring from a cloud of rangy grey-green foliage, and continue to flower for many weeks, especially if spent blooms are removed. When fully out, the colour impact of the flowers is intense, especially when planted in drifts, and the contrast with the finely divided fern-like foliage is always pleasing. At the end of the season the plant develops long, curving seed capsules, tapering to a point at the end – pale green at first and then drying to light brown. These eventually split – if you gently touch a ripe pod you can see this happening – and expel seeds that find their way into all corners of the garden. This is not a shy plant, and it will self-seed freely if given half a chance. Luckily, they seem to look good wherever they appear the following season – in between cracks in paving stones or amongst the leeks and cabbages in a vegetable garden.

> **'A plant of heavenly colour'**
> BETH CHATTO

Although related to the opium poppy (*Papaver somniferum*), the Californian poppy does not have the same narcotic properties. On the contrary, it tends to normalize psychological function rather than disorientate it, and has mildly sedative and antispasmodic properties that are useful particularly in treating children. The native Americans were known to have used sap from the plant as a pain-killer for toothache.

Bloom

The vibrantly coloured, papery flowers grow up to 8cm (3in) in diameter and are cup-like when fully out. On dull days they furl themselves up, as if making a statement against the lack of sun.

Foliage

Growing up to 20cm (8in) long, the feathery, grey-green, deeply cut leaves perform an interesting double act with the flowers, showing them off to perfection.

Seed

The seedheads of the Californian poppy are worth waiting for. The long, narrow pods look attractive among the foliage, and as they dry out they split to reveal tiny round seeds.

Height 30cm (12in)
Spread 15cm (6in)

Cultivation

One of the easiest of all annuals to grow, seed of the Californian poppy should be sown *in situ* in mid-spring or early autumn. Grown in an open, sunny position in average to poor soil, it will need little to no maintenance.

Propagation

Spread seed thinly in short drills, 1cm (½in) deep, and cover with finely raked soil.

Pests and diseases

The plants are not troubled by any pests or diseases.

Associations

Californian poppies are good for planting in generous drifts, filling in holes between other plants. For a big burst of fiery colour, plant with a deep red potentilla such as 'William Robinson'.

Honesty

Lunaria annua

Bud

Honesty's tiny, prolific buds appear in early spring, soon to burst forth into clouds of purple flowers.

Honesty is such an attractive name for a plant that you are automatically well-disposed towards it whether you know it or not. Its flat, silvery seed pods are its trademark, giving the plant both its common and botanical names – lunaria comes from *luna*, meaning moon, relating to the shape of the seed pods, while 'honesty', a name dating back to the sixteenth century, alludes either to the seed pods' resemblance to coins or to their transparent, 'see-through' nature. Because of these associations, the plant is also known by various other common names, including the money plant, moonwort or satin flower. In folklore, the plant had magical properties, used by sorcerers to help people fly, to recover lost things and even to bring the dead back to life. It was also believed that the plant would flourish only in the gardens of those of true and honest character!

'Honesty is the best policy'
PROVERB

A biennial – that is, flowering the year after it has been sown, rather than the same year – honesty is a valuable spring border plant, its delicate but abundant flowers appearing in early spring and lasting into early summer. Various cultivars are available, offering flower colours in purple, pink and white, including a variegated form. When the flowers begin to fade, the round seed pods take their cue – green at first, but soon colouring purple and transforming into shining silver 'coins' that play in the light. The seed pods will eventually expel the round, flat, black seeds, but the case, surprisingly tough, remains intact for many months, even providing company for winter snowdrops. The seeds have a particularly high oil content and contain nervonic acid, essential to the healthy functioning of the human nervous system. In recent years honesty has been grown as a large-scale crop and the seeds used in pharmaceutical experiments.

Bloom

Honesty's small flowers, 1cm (½in) across and consisting of four distinct petals, are grouped together in busy clusters all over the plant. The flowers can be cut to add to informal flower arrangements.

Foliage

Honesty has attractive, heart-shaped, serrated leaves that can grow up to 15cm (6in) long towards the base of the plant.

Seed

Height 90cm (3ft)
Spread 30cm (12in)

Cultivation
Honesty will thrive in sun or shade, and is not fussy about its soil. The seed pods will grow more abundantly, however, if the soil is enriched with manure or compost before sowing.

Propagation
Sow seed *in situ* in spring. Thin seedlings as required.

Pests and diseases
The plant can be affected by clubroot, like other members of the cabbage family. It is also affected by mosaic virus, which manifests itself as white streaks in the purple flowers.

Associations
Honesty looks good in an informal spring border, mixing happily with perennials, bulbs or even in the shade of shrubs. The purple forms mix well with a white tulip such as 'White Triumphator'. Thinking ahead to autumn, the silver seed pods stand out well against a dark-leaved shrub like *Cotinus coggygria* 'Royal Purple'.

Honesty's moon-like oval seed pods provide an attractive focus in the autumn and winter border, and are often used in dried flower arrangements. The discs are made up of three paper-thin layers. Greeny-purple at first, see page 8, when brown the two outer layers can be peeled off to reveal the black seeds which are attached to a silvery central 'partition'. These are eventually expelled, and will produce numerous seedlings the following year.

Sources

Seed suppliers

UK

Chiltern Seeds
Bortree Stile,
Ulverston,
Cumbria LA12 7PB
tel: 01229 581137
www.chilternseeds.co.uk

Samuel Dobie & Son
Long Road,
Paignton,
Devon TQ4 7SX
tel: 01803 696444
www.dobies.co.uk

Mr Fothergill's Seeds
Kentford,
Newmarket,
Suffolk CB8 7QB
tel: 01638 552512
www.mr-fothergills.co.uk

Johnsons Seeds
Gazeley Road,
Kentford,
Newmarket,
Suffolk CB8 7QB
tel: 01638 552200

E. W. King & Co.
Monks Farm,
Coggeshall Road,
Kelvedon,
Essex CO5 9PG
tel: 01376 570000

S. E. Marshall & Co.
Wisbech,
Cambridgeshire PE13 2BR
tel: 01945 583407
www.marshalls-seeds.co.uk

Seeds-by-Size
45 Crouchfield,
Boxmoor,
Hemel Hempstead,
Hertfordshire HP1 1PA
tel: 01442 251458
www.seeds-by-size.co.uk

Suttons
Woodview Road,
Paignton,
Devon TQ4 7NG
tel: 01803 696363
www.suttons.co.uk

Suffolk Herbs
Monks Farm,
Coggeshall Road,
Kelvedon,
Essex CO5 9PG
tel: 01376 572456

Thompson & Morgan
Poplar Lane,
Ipswich,
Suffolk IP8 3BU
tel: 01473 688821
www.thompson-morgan.com

Unwins Seeds
Histon,
Cambridge CB4 4ZZ
tel: 01223 236236
www.unwins-seeds.co.uk

USA & CANADA
Burpee Seeds
Warminster,
Pennsylvania 18974
Freetoll: 001 800 333 5808
www.burpee.com

The Cook's Garden
PO Box 5010,
Hodges,
SC 29653-5010
Freetoll: 001 800 457 9703
www.cooksgarden.com

HPS Seeds
PO Box 10,
571 Whaley Pond Road,
Graniteville,
SC 29829
Freetoll: 001 800 322 7288
www.hpsseed.com

Johnny's Selected Seeds
Foss Hill Road,
Albion,
Maine 04910
tel: 001 207 437 4357
www.johnnyseeds.com

Seeds of Change
PO Box 15700,
Santa Fe,
NM 87506
Freetoll: 001 888 762 7333

Territorial Seed Company
PO Box 157,
Cottage Grove,
OR 97424-0061
tel: 001 541 942 9547
www.territorial-seed.com

The Cottage Gardener
4199 Gilmore Road
RR1 Newtonville
Ontario LOA 1JO
tel: 001 905 786 2388

Useful websites:
www.discoveringannuals.com
www.garden.com

Acknowledgements

I would like to dedicate this book to my friend and neighbour June Rogers for all her help and inspiration in this project, and for caring for my garden in my absence.

Also many thanks to Leslie Forbes, who started the process of turning my idea into a reality; and to Caz and Clare whose design and words have given it life, with much help from Muna and all the crew at Conran. Last, but not least, love and thanks to my partner Shaun, for all his encouragement and input.

Carol Sharp
www.carolsharp.co.uk

Thanks to the following sources for use of quotes: Page 11: Select Seeds website, www.selectseeds.com. Page 19: Shakespeare's Sonnet No. 116. Page 27: quote from list of quotations on www.angelfire.com. Page 35: Discovering Annuals by Graham Rice, published by Frances Lincoln, 1999. Reproduced by permission of Frances Lincoln Ltd, 4 Torriano Mews, Torriano Avenue, London NW5 2RZ. Page 43: from the poem Justina and the Nightingale by Percy Bysshe Shelley. Page 51: from Epistle I by Alexander Pope. Page 59: Christopher Lloyd's Garden Flowers by Christopher Lloyd, published by Cassell & Co, 2000. Page 75: Beth Chatto's Gravel Garden by Beth Chatto, published by Frances Lincoln, 2000. Reproduced by permission of Frances Lincoln Ltd, 4 Torriano Mews, Torriano Avenue, London NW5 2RZ.

Every effort has been made to trace the copyright holders and we apologise in advance for any unintentional omissions and would be pleased to insert the appropriate acknowledgement in any subsequent publication.